Sri Ramakrishna (1836-1886) and a nineteenth century subaltern: Rani Rashmoni (1793-1861). Creating our feminist genealogies.
The unholy alliance between gender and religion.

TAPATI BHARADWAJ

ISBN: 8192875229
ISBN-13: 978-8192875224

DEDICATION

Religion and gender in India make unwilling partners and are often seen as having irreconcilable differences. We desire to make bridges in the hope that religion can aid in empowering women and join hands in becoming part of the feminist movement. We desire to hope that our daughters achieve parity through and within institutionalized religion.

CONTENTS

ACKNOWLEDGMENTS

My journey in wondering what a feminist genealogy in the Indian context would look like started during my graduate study in the Women's Studies department at the University of Cincinnati. Subsequently, one winter and spring, I found myself at Lahore, at the Institute of Women's Studies. That was eons ago, and what seems like a lifetime later, I found myself at the end of that journey.

Tapati Bharadwaj.

1 INTRODUCTION.

The turn of the nineteenth century is murky in its details of how women lived, loved (if at all), raised children and died. If we want to trace the circumstances under which women lived in the immediate years after the presence of the East India Company, we do not really have much to bank upon due to a paucity of primary sources and narratives that were written about women at this time period. The common thread that emerges is that women were safely oppressed within the patriarchal mould. In *Women Writing in India, 600 BC to the Present*, the editors introduce Rassundari Devi's autobiography, *Amar Jiboni*, which was published in 1867, as symptomizing all these facets.[1] Rassundari Devi was born in a small village in Bengal in 1810 and was married quite early. The editors write that the book was an "astonishing achievement" of sorts, considering the extremely harsh conditions under which she wrote:[2]

> [this was a work of an] ordinary housewife who had taught herself to read and write in secret by scratching the letters of the alphabet onto a corner of the blackened kitchen wall. Yet her Bengali prose is so crisp and readable that it could be mistaken for modern text. ...
>
> Some of the most moving parts of her account describe her struggle to escape the grind of a petty domesticity and teach herself how to read and write.
>
> ... The tone [of the narrative] typical of Rassundari's writing is one of understatement and restraint, but what emerges is a clear

---

[1] "Introduction" to *Rassundari Devi*, in *Women Writing in India: 600 BC to the Present, Vol. I*. eds. Susie Tharu and K. Lalitha (New York: Feminist Press of the City University of New York, 1991), pp. 190-192.

[2] Ibid., pp.190-192.

Sri Ramakrishna (1836-1886) and a nineteenth century subaltern.

indictment of the way Bengali society in her time treated women like her. [3]

The dominant trope that emerges, not only in primary texts like Rassundari Devi's *Amar Jiboni* but even in feminist scholarship which looks at the lives of women of the nineteenth century, is that of the oppressed woman and this is reasonably justifiable.

Another recurring theme that emerges in writings of this time period is that of sati – and this much, though, we can say is that the issue of sati was a major political sword which was wielded both by the newly arrived English rulers and the natives. The implication was that the condition of native women was deplorable, at the most. For example, in a petition against sati, Raja Rammohun Roy wrote to Lord Bentick in 1830, the then governor general of India about the practise and applauding the legal steps taken by the British government:

> …we the undersigned Native inhabitants of Calcutta and its vicinity, [acknowledge] the protection which [the British government] has recently afforded to the lives of the Hindoo female part of your subjects and for your humane and successful exertions in rescuing us forever, from the gross stigma hitherto attached to our character, as wilful murderers of females and zealous promoters of the practise of suicide.

This was a facet of Bengali society at that time period, but as we slowly recuperate stories and narratives of women who were living in the nineteenth century, we see that sometimes, it is possible to create a different picture where not all women were absolutely relegated to the realm of the private and domestic.

How do we go about this intellectual and feminist business of finding a tradition of our immediate foremothers that is outside the overwhelmingly dominant notion of the oppressed woman, considering the paucity of documented histories or personal narratives? – and by immediate past, I refer to the time period just around when the East India Company was establishing itself as rulers of India. When the Britishers arrived, were all native women victims? It is within this premise that I try to understand the life of Rani Rashmoni (1793-1861), who can be considered as actively involved not only in philanthropy but also in business and management. She was born in a poor family, in a village near Calcutta. Eventually, she became a well known female entrepreneur and philanthropist of the early-

---

[3] Ibid., pp. 190-192.

mid nineteenth century in Bengal. She is largely remembered now as having
built the Kali temple at Dakshineshwar and as being the patron of Sri
Ramakrishna (1836-1886), the mystic saint from Bengal. Her wealth was
amassed due to business with the Britishers. The fact that she was a *shudra*,
a lower caste woman, seemed to have aided her in gaining entry in the
public realm, an opportunity otherwise denied to upper caste women.
Overtly, she conformed to all patriarchal norms of the early-mid nineteenth
century– and within this garb of religion and domesticity, she was able to
engage with the public world. A narrative on Rani Rashmoni from Swami
Chetananda's *They Lived With God* describes her day to day activities in the
following manner:[4]

> In spite of her responsibility now as owner and custodian of such
> immense wealth, [after the death of her husband] Rashmoni remained
> as unattached as ever. According to Hindu custom widows do not
> remarry. They lead a pure and unattached life like a nun. Rashmoni
> also followed the ancient tradition. Early in the morning, she would
> get up and repeat the mantram in the shrine. Then in midmorning she
> would sit in her office and sign documents, appoint officers, check
> accounts, and discuss various problems and projects with Mathur [her
> son-in-law who assisted her]. At noon she would partake of the food
> which had been offered to the Lord, and then she would rest. Later in
> the day, after supervising the office work, she would attend the vesper.
> She was fond of inviting Brahmin scholars and listening to their
> discourses on the scriptures.[5]

In this description on Rani Rashmoni's life, there is an easy to and fro
movement between the private life of a religious widow and the public
world of business. It is at the interstices of the interiority of her life, and the
public-ness of being a member of the rich elite that we have to deconstruct
her life. Her life is a counter discourse to the norm; and the conundrum is
this: why did Sri Ramakrishna allow her to be his patron and in the process
legitimate the participation of a woman in a public life – a role that was
mostly denied to all women at this time period?

In the popular imagination of an average Bengali, or an Indian,
Rani Rashmoni is a well known figure, and yet, in any narrative on feminist
theory or history on nineteenth century women in India, she rarely makes

---

[4] Swami Chetananda, "Rani Rasmani" in *They Lived With God, Life Stories of Some Devotees of Sri Ramakrishna* (Calcutta: Advaita Ashram, 1999), pp. 1-16.

[5] Ibid., p. 7.

Sri Ramakrishna (1836-1886) and a nineteenth century subaltern.

her presence felt. Her elision, wilful erasure, in feminist scholarship is a bit of a mystery. There is a plethora of literature on her, courtesy most writings that emerge from the Ramakrishna Mission. Why have feminist historians, scholars and writers, though, refused to engage with her? Is religion a taboo word to feminist theory? Is it because Rani Rashmoni is seen as an intrinsic figure in Sri Ramakrisha's life that feminists have avoided confronting her in theory? More importantly, the life of Rani Rashmoni compels us to go beyond the usual trajectory of how oppressively women lived in the early nineteenth century. We are, therefore, compelled to arrive at new interpretative models which will allow us to sift out from within such primary sources like narratives on religion about the lives of women who were both within and without the patriarchal, brahmanical fold.

2 ON SATI AND OTHER FEMINIST ISSUES: DEBATING ABOUT THE SUBALTERN.

A dominant image that emerges from the early nineteenth century in India is that of the victimized woman; oppressed as a result of patriarchy or religion. In "Contentious Traditions:: The Debate on Sati in Colonial India,"[6] Lata Mani writes that the abolition of sati by the British in 1829 was "a founding moment in the history of women in modern India" whereby "women became the site on which tradition was debated."[7] The legislative prohibition of sati was the culmination of a debate during which 8134 instances of sati had been recorded, mostly among upper caste Hindus, with a high concentration – 63 percent – in the area around Calcutta. Therefore, we who are situated in the present, who look at the historical past, have been compelled to acknowledge the benevolence of British rule.[8] Mani's interest is in the discursive aspects of the debate,[9] which makes her argue that under colonial rule, "women become emblematic of tradition" and these notions of tradition were negotiated upon by "debating the rights and status of women in society."[10] This version of colonial discourse was a result of colonial interaction with select natives, who considered brahmanical Hinduism as the authentic version of Hinduism and therefore, brahmanical scripture as privileged, whereby tradition was equated with this scriptural knowledge.[11]

---

[6] Lata Mani, "Contentious Traditions: The Debate on *Sati* in Colonial India" in *Recasting Women, Essays in Colonial History* (New Delhi: Kali for Women, 1997), pp. 88-126.

[7] Ibid., p. 118.

[8] Ibid., p. 88.

[9] Ibid., 89.

[10] Ibid., p. 90.

[11] Ibid., p. 90.

Sri Ramakrishna (1836-1886) and a nineteenth century subaltern.

But was sati of such immense relevance at that time period, affecting all women? Can we not say that this was but one facet of Bengali society at that time period, which undoubtedly was misogynous to say the least, and as we slowly recuperate stories and narratives of other lives, we see a different picture evolving, where not all women were absolutely relegated to the realm of the oppressive private and domestic. It is within this premise that I try to understand the life of Rani Rashmoni, who can be considered as actively involved not only in philanthropy but also in business, despite overtly conforming to patriarchal and caste norms. Such a perspective will allow us a more nuanced notion of the lives of women in the early –mid nineteenth century – and nudge us into going beyond absolute binaries of black and white.

Redefining conventional sources for feminist histories.

Tracing and understanding the lives of 19th century women in India is an uphill task; it is possible to unearth the lives of these women if we are able to look beyond the conventional textual sources? How do we find primary sources and textual narratives which will allow us to rewrite the stories of women who lived in the nineteenth century? Rani Rashmoni's life is very clearly mentioned in all the narratives that look at the life of Sri Ramakrishna.

Sri Ramakrishna was born in 1836, in Kamarpukur, a small village around sixty miles from Calcutta. His brother, Ramkumar, moved to Calcutta in 1850, and opened a school. In 1852, Ramakrishna followed him and assisted him. In 1855, when Ramkumar became the priest of the Dakshineshwar temple, whose patron was Rani Rashmoni, Ramakrishna joined him and it was here that he lived most of his adult life. Was Sri Ramakrishna more a closeted social revolutionary than anything else, and through his politics of allowing for a lower caste woman to be his patron, articulating a position that was socially radical? In the early nineteenth century, through the life of Rani Rashmoni, we do get to hear the subaltern speak, thus problematizing the feminist conundrum – can the subaltern speak?

Why is the subaltern silenced?

Feminist scholars have been concerned about the female subaltern's silence as it reflects a negation of agency. The common theory is that the silence of the subaltern is a result of her being unable to understand the heightened level of exploitation by global capitalism, patriarchy and the narratives of imperialism. Gayatri Spivak's repeated demand to hear the "voice-consciousness" of the subaltern is a result of her realization that other agencies have tended to speak for the subaltern, making her conclude that the "subaltern cannot speak".[12] Elsewhere, a similar desire to grapple with what the subaltern has to say is evident when Spivak writes, "no amount of raised-consciousness fieldwork can even approach the painstaking labor [needed] to establish ethical singularity with the subaltern." Sri Ramakrishna was able to achieve this kind of "ethical singularity" with the subaltern. Moreover, Rani Rashmoni's life is a self representation by a nineteenth century subaltern, which reveals a heightened degree of self awareness and critical consciousness.

The impossibility of subaltern representation: the debate on subalternity.

Postcolonial feminist scholars have voiced their concern at the existing scholarship which depicts third world women (hereafter referred to as the subaltern) to the world. According to them, subaltern representation is, under most circumstances, impossible and if possible, then self-representation by the subaltern is also an essential aspect which they claim to be lacking. This epistemological position thwarts the intellectuals attempts at knowledge construction about the subaltern. What is often forgotten is that the discursive, i.e. theorization about the subaltern, affects the way we think about the material and the agenda of numerous government and development bodies (like the IMF and World Bank). Oftentimes, as in development scholarship, women of the richer North formulate strategies which affect the lifestyles of women of the poorer South. In this instance, their knowledge is not more epistemically truthful, but more powerful and compelling because of the

---

[12] Gayatri Spivak, "Translator's Preface and Afterword to Mahasweta Devi's Imaginary Maps" in *The Spivak Reader*, eds. Donna Landry and Gerald McLean (New York: Routledge, 1996), pp. 267-286; "Subaltern Talk: Interview with the Editors" in *The Spivak Reader*, pp. 287-308; "Theory in the Margin: Coetze's Foe Reading Defoe's Crusoe/ Roxana" in *Consequences of Theory: Selected Papers from the English Institute*, 1987-88, eds. Jonathan Arac and Barbara Johnson (Baltimore: The John Hopkins University Press, 1991), pp. 154-181; "Can The Subaltern Speak?" in *Marxism and the Interpretation of Culture*, eds. Cary Nelson and Lawrence Grossberg (Urbana: University of Illinois Press, 1988), pp. 271-313; *In Other Worlds: Essays in Cultural Politics* (London: Methuen, 1987); "The Rani of Sirmur" in *Europe and Its Others*, eds. Francis Barker et al. (Colchester: University of Essex Press, 1985), pp. 128-151.

location of those who produce it. This is what is to be discussed in this section — under what circumstances has it been possible to empower the subaltern?

How do we account for discourses which are constructed not as a result of the subaltern's vocalization but are, nonetheless, emancipatory in nature? By differentiating between 'intellectual' and 'subaltern' consciousness, I argue that in some instances, 'outsiders' have a perspective which is denied to the subaltern which allows for emancipatory knowledge construction. Here, the notion of 'ethics' emerges as the common theme which has the potential to disrupt what is often an assumed perception; that subaltern representation is always flawed. The apparent absence of reasons as to why a non-subaltern would be involved at all haunts both the native and first world scholars, which can be explained away by espousing an ethical stance. If the feminist agenda aims at ensuring socially just systems, those in powerful positions have not only to be aware of their involvement in perpetuating this system but subsequently, through constant interrogation, transmute their involvement into a benevolent one.

What was it that allowed and motivated Sri Ramakrishna to allow Rani Rashmoni to be his patron – if not the notion of "ethical singularity"? He was very conscious of the fact that he was a brahmin; he was present alongside his brother Ramkumar Chatterjee at the dedication ceremony at the Kali temple at Dakshineshwar. But he did not eat any of the offered food, and instead ate puffed rice which he bought on his way back to Calcutta – where he was staying with his brother. We cannot elide the fact that Rani Rashmoni belonged to the lower caste. Despite Sri Ramakrishna's initial hesitation at the fact that his brother was involved in the functioning of this temple, Ramakrishna eventually did assist his brother and by doing so, interrogated his own upper caste social position. In this particular instance, Ramakrishna was in a position of superiority and was a non-subaltern, but that he did align with Rani Rashmoni – in many ways -- reflects his capacity to undo his position of power. He did thwart the caste hierarchy, and in the process, was involved in ensuring that he did not perpetuate a system of oppression. This allowed Rani Rashmoni to define herself as a subject and an agent, very much akin to the imperial subject.

Interrogating subaltern knowledge: defining the subaltern subject.

Discourses of postmodernism have been responsible for critiquing the imperial subject by arguing that the unity of this subject was possible only at the expense of the racial, ethnic and feminine object. Subsequently, a large body of scholarship influenced by postmodernism, has been involved in the process of transmuting the racial, ethnic feminine object into subjects. A common allegation which is cast at this scholarship is that the valorization of the third world woman (also synonymous with the subaltern woman) is beset with misrepresentations. Gayatri Spivak, by closely examining imperialist representation, demonstrates how knowledge is produced in the service of colonialist appropriation. She has referred to the systemic workings of representation and silencing that is evident in the feminist scholarship which depicts third world women to the world and is true of both 'western' and native scholars.' Spivak's trenchant critique of 'feminists and native informants who occupy subject positions, states that they are incapable of referring to the third world subaltern woman without patronage or presumption.[13] Being involved in cultural studies, these scholars are involved in the politics of representation.[14] The solution which Spivak arrives at is to foreground the native subaltern woman whose self representation can rectify the past (mis) representations. As the imperial subject defines the subaltern as the other and uses her to complement the rational(western) self, demands are made that the subaltern woman represent herself in a similar fashion. The subaltern is conceptualized as possessing a critical consciousness which would enable her to define herself in the same fashion as the imperial subject or the native informant. For example, Spivak demands that first world feminists should stop "feeling privileged as a woman."[15] when they describe the third world women. Therefore, they should ask, "not merely who am I? but who is the other woman? How am I naming her? How does she name me?"[16] By overlooking an obvious difference between the 'I' and the 'she,' Spivak makes invisible the fact that the sophisticated academic and the subaltern 'other' inhabit dissimilar social, geographical and intellectual environments which affect the very manner in which they conceptualize the 'self and 'other'. Moreover, this Spivak-ian exercise can be performed only if both the researcher and participant are equal; as the subaltern consciousness is different from the consciousness of

---

[13] The native informant has been defined as the "curious guardian at the margin"(Spivak, "Theory in the Margin," p. 172) who exists for "first world intellectuals interested in the other"(Spivak, "Can the Subaltern Speak," p. 284). Her entry into the western academia is a product of the process "by which the putative center welcomes selective inhabitants of the margins in order to better exclude the margin"(Spivak, *In Other Worlds*, p. 107).
[14] According to Spivak, there is a tendency to "think of the third world as distant cultures, exploited but with rich intact heritages waiting to be recovered, interpreted, and curricularized in English translation"(Spivak, "The Rani of Sirmur," p. 128). She is aware of the difficulty in "fixing such a signifier as an object of knowledge"(p. 128).

[15] Spivak, *In Other Worlds*, p. 136.

[16] Ibid., p. 150.

Sri Ramakrishna (1836-1886) and a nineteenth century subaltern.

the intellectual, such a situation is near impossible.

In "Can The Subaltern Speak," Spivak begins with a critique of "those intellectuals who are our best prophets of heterogeneity and the Other,[17]" her targets being Foucault and Deleuze. The element of doubt which is evident in her writings is a result of her disbelief in their objective of wanting to create conditions whereby the oppressed would be able to speak for themselves.[18] The western intellectual desires to retrieve the consciousness of the oppressed in isolation from "the palimpsets narrative of imperialism"[19] in his "positing" of "an unrepresentable subaltern subject that can know and speak itself " thus allowing "him" to "abstain from representation."[20] By conjuring up the "lost figure of the colonized"[21] the intellectual constructs a "homogeneous Other referring to (his) own place in the Seat of the Same or the Self."[22] These are attempts to concretize ways of defining the subaltern consciousness. But because of the international division of labor, the subaltern has been a by-product of the modes of production rather than a subject with her own autonomy. There is "no space from which the sexed subaltern subject can speak" as she is shuttled between "tradition and modernization."[23]

Intellectuals who believe that the subaltern can represent herself are ignorant of the fact that she exists "on the other side of the international division of labor from socialized capital, inside and outside the circuit of the epistemic violence of imperialist law and education supplementing an earlier economic text."[24] Spivak arrives at the conclusion that the voice of the subaltern cannot be heard in the text of imperialism nor in that of insurgency. Spivak's repeated demand to hear the "voice-consciousness" of the subaltern is a result of her realization that other agencies have tended to speak for the subaltern, making her conclude that the "subaltern cannot speak".

---

[17] "Can the Subaltern Speak," p. 272.

[18] Ibid., p. 274.

[19] Ibid., p. 281.

[20] Ibid., 285.

[21] Ibid., p. 295.

[22] Ibid., p. 288.

[23] Ibid., p. 307.

[24] Ibid., p. 283.

Elsewhere, a similar desire to grapple with what the subaltern has to say is evident when Spivak writes, "no amount of raised-consciousness fieldwork can even approach the painstaking labor [needed] to establish ethical singularity with the subaltern."[25] To her, an "ethical singularity" bears the implication that there should be responses from both sides (implying the subaltern and the academic) which includes "responsibility and accountability."[26] She goes on to elaborate on the failure of political movements and concludes that such social movements rarely happen because of the absence of such kinds of engagement. It is impossible for those initiating to "engage every subaltern in this way, especially across gender lines," and therefore, "ethics is the experience of the impossible."[27] But, when one tries to interact with the subaltern, within this ethical framework, she acknowledges the possibility of the difficult truth, that "internalised gendering perceived as ethical choice is the hardest roadblock for women.... The only way to break it is by establishing an ethical singularity with the woman in question, itself a necessary supplement to a collective action to which the woman might offer resistance, passive or active."[28] It is, therefore, not possible for one to have a dialogue. Though Spivak moves from the statement that the subaltern has not been given the space to speak to commenting on the difficulty involved in having a conversation with her, the central focus still remains on the agency and voice of the subaltern.

Locating the lives of the subaltern: where do we go?

The focus here is to retrieve the voice of a nineteenth century subaltern and the conditions under which she lived. By having a dialogue with a subject from the past, by recuperating a history that has been elided by feminist historians, we are compelled to conclude that Rani Rashmoni was an agent on her own rights. Oftentimes, we have to be willing to venture into documented sources out of the norm in order to create a space from where we can make ethical contact with the subaltern. even if the subaltern seems not to have any agency – complying and conforming to most norms of patriarchy, caste and class. We have to create new interpretative parameters to read within and into the stories which create these social matrices that construct the oppressed female subaltern. More importantly, where do we

[25] Spivak, "Translator's Preface," p. 269.

[26] Ibid., pp. 269-270.

[27] Ibid., p. 270.

[28] Ibid., p. 272.

Sri Ramakrishna (1836-1886) and a nineteenth century subaltern.

locate primary or even secondary material about women who lived at this time period? If we, as feminists, are willing to broaden our focus on what texts we are willing to read, then we can sketch out the lives of women who were living at this time period. It is because of Sri Ramakrishna that we know so much about the life of Rani Rashmoni but why is it that we hear little about her, or there is little mention of her, outside the works published on Sri Ramakrishna by the Ramakrishna Mission?

3 RECUPERATING A SUBALTERN LIFE: RANI RASHMONI.

In the early nineteenth century, Vaishnavite women in Bengal were often literate; more importantly, they were involved in a lot of what we would refer to as performative art and education. They were traveling mendicants and public perfomers (*Boshtomis*) in the newly established city of Calcutta[29] and were also involved in teaching the women of the *andarmahal* through *kathakatha*. Swarnakumari Devi, the older sister of Rabindranath Tagore recounts a story of a Vaishnav woman who would teach those in the *andarmahal*:

> A Vaishnavite lady – pure after a bath, dressed in white, fair-skinned – appeared in the zenana to teach. She was no mean scholar. She was well versed in Sanskrit, and needless to say, in Bengali also. Moreover, she had a wonderful power of describing, and impressed everyone with her kathakata performance. Even those who were not in the least interested in learning, used to gather at the reading room to listen to the Vaishnavite lady's description of the dawn, of gods and goddesses.[30]

Swarnakumrai Devi was born in 1855, and this incident took place earlier. What we find here is a different portrayal about women who lived in the early nineteenth century, and this narrative is outside the usual dominant norm of sati, polygamy and female emancipation. The Vaishnavite woman is not named by the writer, and her anonymity symbolizes in many ways all the unnamed women who would have been educated but who have been elided in history. For that matter, we take for granted that most women would have been illiterate. For us, the interest is in establishing a feminist genealogy of sorts – and maybe, these women were the precursors of the

---

[29] See Sumanta Sarkar, "Marginalization of Women's Popular Culture in Nineteenth Century Bengal" in *Recasting Women: Essays in Colonial History*, eds. Kumkum Sangari and Sudesh Vaid (New Delhi: Kali for Women, 1997), pp. 127-179.

[30] Cited in Sumit Sarkar, Ibid., p. 151.

present and maybe, these unnamed, literate Vaishnav women were partial agents on their own – even while conforming to the patriarchal norms. It is within this tradition that we have to understand Rani Rashmoni, who was born in a Vaishnav community.

Rani Rashmoni

Rani Rashmoni was born in 1793, in a village near Calcutta. Her parents were peasants, mostly involved in agriculture and other labor associated with village life.[31] Her father would also repair the roofs of the houses in the village. Rani Rashmoni's childhood was as usual for young children of her background; she was involved in the household economy of assisting her mother. She would carry food to his father, and help in picking vegetables from the kitchen garden. There is no documented source which underlies Swami Chetananda's account of her early life, unless it be that this written account is through hearsay or from accepted knowledge of how life for a young poor girl from a lower caste background would have been in the late eighteenth century. She was fond of swinging from a hammock which was tied to a mango tree. Despite being a farmer, Rani Rashmoni's father, Harekrishna, was literate and taught her how to read and write. He was also a village storyteller and involved in "spreading mass education."[32] In the evenings, the village would listen to his "melodious and dramatic" renditions from the Mahabharata and the Ramayana. Her parents were devout Vaishnavas and Rani Rashmoni would play act being a Vaishnava.

This allows us a glimpse into subaltern life; how did lower caste women live in rural Bengal at the end of the eighteenth century? How were they perceived by their family members? To what extent were they educated? The significance of the fact that Rani Rashmoni's family were Vasihnavas is this: Rani Rashmoni's family, despite being poor, lower caste and involved in an agrarian economy, were literate and it seemed to be acceptable for women to be educated. Her life does not follow the usual trajectory where she was completely deprived of an education, and had to learn her alphabets in a painstaking manner, eavesdropping while her brothers were taught. Was her life the norm for many other women who were living at this time period?

She was married at the age of eleven, to the son of a rich landlord from Calcutta, Rajchandra Das. Her father in law, Pritaram, was a self made

---

[31] For more on her life, see "Rani Rashmoni" in Swami Chetananda's *They Lived with God, Life Stories of Some Devotees of Sri Ramakrishna* (Calcutta: Advaita Ashram, 1989), pp. 1-16.

[32] Ibid., p. 3.

man, who was a clerk in a salt distributing agency in Calcutta and then became a manager of a large estate in Bangladesh. Subsequently, he became an independent entrepreneur in Calcutta, and a supplier of goods to the East India Company, developing a "close relationship" with them.[33]

Pritaram died in 1817, and Rajchandra inherited his estate, which comprised of 650,000 rupees and large amounts of property. Rajchandra and Rashmoni were involved in a lot of philanthropy and social work. In this particular narrative on her life, she emerges as being a social equal to her husband in many respects as a result of her involvement with charity and being an agent in determining how to use money for philanthropy. To what extent was Rani Rashmoni a silenced subaltern of the early nineteenth century? Rajchandra was a member of the elite of Calcutta, as it was turning out to be a newly established city for the Britishers; he was friends with Prince Dwarakanath Tagore, Akrur Dutta, Kaliprasanna Sinha, Sir Raja Radhakanta Deb, Lord Auckland, John Bebb and others. We learn about Rajchandra through narratives that are written on Rani Rashmoni; we learn that he was quite on friendly terms with the Britishers and also very honest – he kept his promise to his brother in law to lend an insolvent British merchant ten thousand rupees. If Rani Rashmoni was closely involved with him, (and this we can assume as she easily fitted into the role of manager of his estates once he died), she would also have been very cognizant of the larger cosmopolitan world Rajchandra belonged to – of the native elites, the British rulers and traders, and the larger native population.

It was possible for Rani Rashmoni to blend in the simplicity and Vaishnavism of her early childhood with the opulent newness of the city of Calcutta. A telling example of her capacity to negotiate with and against the dominant socio-cultural presence of the Britisher is evident in the choice she made; in 1838 (two years after the death of her husband), she had a desire to celebrate the Car Festival and Mathur was asked to build a silver chariot to carry Lord Krishna. A British company, Hamilton, was suggested but Rani Rashmoni was against this and instead wanted local silversmiths to be hired so that they could be patronized. Devotees thronged the festival and a separate banquet was arranged for foreign dignitaries.[34] She took pains to ensure that local craftsmen were patronized and their professional skills were retained and at the same time, wooed the British rulers by making them participants of this religious procession. What is an unexplained phenomenon but would be remarkable is the ease with which

---

[33] Ibid., p. 4.
[34] Ibid., p. 7.

Sri Ramakrishna (1836-1886) and a nineteenth century subaltern.

she made transitions from one episteme to another, reconciling quite different world views.

To understand Rani Rashmoni, we have to understand the larger socio-cultural context from within which she was functioning. What made it possible for her to confidently operate in the public world as an entrepreneur? To what extent was she a silenced subaltern? It is possible to argue that she would not have immune from the influences of her husband and her son in law, who were participants in the larger socio-cultural changes that were taking place in Calcutta. Her acumen in business and legal theory could be a result of this engagement. Calcutta at this time period of 1814, was a city that had sprung up out of three small villages, and within a few decades had grown to become a Westernised, multi-lingual urban space. The British had utilised many aspects of Western civilization in making the city. What was the nature of this newly established geo-social space where Rani Rashmoni grew to become an astute businesswoman and a patron of religion – building the Kali temple where Sri Ramakrishna would become the head priest. It would not have been an easy task for her, negotiating with the Britishers and the Bengali *bhadraloks* and *zamindars*, despite being assisted by Mathur Biswas. Calcutta, in the early years of the nineteenth century was a space which saw a vast array of people. In order to comprehensively understand her world, we have to look at the larger picture of the Calcutta.

Tapati Bharadwaj.

4 AN EMERGING COSMOPOLITAN CITY: CALCUTTA AND RANI RASHMONI AS A HYBRID SUBJECT.

Rani Rashmoni as a hybrid subject and her entry into the public world.

Rani Rashmoni was both within and without the socio-religious systems that existed in the early decades of the nineteenth century in Calcutta. Her private life was extremely religious, in keeping with the Vaishnav tradition from within which she emerged, while she seems to have been quite adept in comprehending and understanding how the public world functioned. Thus, what is remarkable in Rani Rashmoni is her capacity of amalgamate many worldviews – she had grown up in a poor, but reasonably educated Vaishnavite community in a village in Bengal, and eventually lived the large part of her life in a city that was becoming westernized in many respects and was constantly changing.

It would be myopic if we elided the fact that she was a part of the cosmopolitan landscape of this newly established city, even if she was not an active participant in all aspects of it. In most narratives on Rani Rashmoni, we do learn about her strict adherence to religion, her simplicity and humility despite her wealth, her astute sense of business and her involvement in building the Kali temple and full faith in Sri Ramakrishna. What we do not read in these narratives but we can conjecture, considering her social context, is her absolute knowledge of the socio-cultural and epistemic changes that were going on in Calcutta. More importantly, and is of great relevance in this particular context, is the fact that she could, with great sophistication, easily blend vastly different social locations. A point of comparison would be to look at the life of another contemporary of hers – Rammohun Roy, who traversed a journey quite similar to the one she made but who also had a very different life.

Sri Ramakrishna (1836-1886) and a nineteenth century subaltern.

Rammohun Roy.

Rammohun was born in 1772 (many regard his date of birth as 1774), in Radhanagar, near Krishnanagar, in a devout Hindu family and inherited the religiosity that marked his forefathers.[35] Krishnanagar was known to be steeped in Hindu culture. His forefathers settled in Murshidabad and were in the service of the Muslim rulers. As a young man, Rammohun was educated in Bengali, and later Persian as the latter was the official language. We can speculate that his education would have been a model of how many young men would have been educated. He was sent to Patna to learn Arabic, where he was taught from Arabic translations of Euclid and Aristotle, the Koran, and the writings of the Sufis. Subsequently, he studied Sanskrit at Benares. He studied in five different languages, namely, Sanskrit, Arabic, Persian, Urdu and Bengali.

By the age of fifteen he was critical of idolatory and left home, traveling to Tibet in order to learn about Buddhism. On his return home after a few years, around 1791-92, he was unable to reconcile himself to the beliefs of his family, and had theological disagreements with them. By 1796 he had separated from his family, and stayed for a while in Calcutta. He also purchased property in Hooghly, which gave him a steady income. As a result of his moneylending practice he interacted with many officials of the East India Company. He left Calcutta in 1799 and traveled in north India, spending some time in Benares. He studied Sanskrit, and earned a living by copying manuscripts. His father died in 1803 and by 1805, he had started working for the East India Company as a *munshi* in Rangpur; his employer was John Digby. It was here that he started to have socio-religious discussions with his native friends. By 1814, when he moved to Calcutta, he had amassed enough money to become a zamindar that allowed him an annual income of ten thousand rupees.[36] His wealth and his moneylending made him superficially indistinguishable from many of the *zamindars* who lived in Calcutta.

Rammohun, though, was different from his contemporaries. By the time he was twenty, he had broken away from the religious tradition of his father, and was thoroughly familiar with Hindu, Islamic and Buddhist systems of thought. He had started life with the intention of working for

---

[35] For the life of Rammohun Roy, see Sophia Dobson Collet, *The Life and Letters of Raja Rammohun Roy*, ed. Dilip Kumar Biswas and Prabhat Chandra Ganguli (Calcutta: Sadharon Brahmo Samaj, 1900). Reprint 1988.

[36] For details on his life, see Collet, *Raja Rammohun Roy*, pp. 1-27.

the Muslim rulers in Murshidabad, but realized that the Islamic phase of
Indian history was on the wane. Rammohun himself had been deeply
rooted in the cosmopolitan upper class Persian culture of the eighteenth
century[37] but with the consolidation of British power in India, Rammohun
and many of his generation of the early nineteenth century alienated
themselves from their Islamic heritage. Moreover, English education
"placed an impenetrable barrier between the nineteenth century and the
immediate pre-British past, which perhaps had contained certain healthy
non-conformist elements along with much that was undoubtedly
ossified."[38] The absence of pre British Islamic scholarship was a result of
the rapid disappearance of the knowledge of Persian, and the emergence of
English historiography.[39]

It is easy to argue that Rammohun was unusual for his time period
in the early nineteenth century; he was like, and unlike, many of his social
contemporaries. Rammohun Roy was forty one years old when he settled in
Calcutta, becoming a member of the nouveau riche. The milieu of rich
families in Calcutta, which emerged in the early years of the East India
Company, represents not merely the economic growth of a particular group
of people, but also has to be seen as a new socio-cultural phenomenon.
According to Chitra Deb, the wealth of the "great houses" was not based
on hereditary occupations or feudal landed wealth; their roots could be
traced to the city of Calcutta, in the years after 1742, during the decline of
the Mughals, when Calcutta grew to become a trading center.[40] Many of the
"great houses" came from the lower castes, and took up posts as
intermediaries between the Indians and the British—in conducting trade,
collecting debts and looking after the accounts of the EIC. Most of them
won enormous wealth through private trade and usury. Rammohun had
also made his wealth through usury, but he distinguished himself from this
social group as he was more of a *pandit* than a *babu*.

Rammohun was well versed in Sanskrit, a scholar in his own right, and
a polyglot. His personal habits were like the *bhadrolok* and yet he hankered

[37] Sushobhan Sarkar, *Notes on the Bengal Renaissance* (Papyrus, 1979), p. 19.

[38] Ibid., p. 18.

[39] Ibid., p. 20.

[40] Chitra Deb, "The Great Houses of Calcutta" *Calcutta: The Living City. Volume I: The Past*,
ed. Sukanta Chaudhuri (Calcutta: Oxford University Press, 1990), pp. 56-63.

for recognition as a shastric scholar. He was "ridiculed by the pandit establishment for imitating the outward appearance of the *ashraf* (Mughal aristocrat) which was fashionable among the *bhadrolok*; he sought scholarly recognition."[41] The *bhadroloks* were Hindus, but they were influenced by the Persianized *nawabi* culture.[42] Though Rammohun would attire himself in a *nawabi* manner, he was quite anglicized in his European habits, and could speak fluent English. He was described by the missionaries in the following manner:

> Rama-Mohana-Raya, a very rich Rarhee[sic] Brahmun of Calcutta, is a respectable Sanskrit scholar, and so well versed in Persian, that he is called Moulvee-Rama-Mohana-Raya: he also writes English with correctness and reads with ease—English, Mathematical and metaphysical works. He has published, in Bengalee, one or two philosophical works from the Sanskrit which he hopes may be useful in leading his countrymen to renounce idolatory. Europeans breakfast at his house, at a separate table in the English fashion; he has paid us a visit at Serampore.[43]

Rammohun was a Sanskrit scholar, who was addressed as a *maulvi*, and also conformed to the prevalent notions of caste.

Even if we never read about Rammohun Roy alongside Rajchandra, Rani Rashmoni or Mathur Biswas, they were all inhabitants of the same world and would have, directly or indirectly, interacted with each other. He would have been a contemporary of Rani Rashmoni, and in many ways, the socio-cultural and epistemic shifts that he made in his life is akin to the manner in which Rani Rashmoni also shifted geo-social and intellectual spaces. To fully comprehend the extent to which she used her intellect to engage with the public world, one has to understand her world – Calcutta as it was in the early nineteenth century.

---

[41] Bruce Carlisle Robertson, *Raja Rammohun Roy. The Father of Modern India.* (Delhi: Oxford University Press, 1999), p. 24.

[42] Till the early nineteenth century, Hindus and Muslims participated in a common elite culture, but differed in how they reacted to British presence. Muslim response was largely negative as they were losing the positions of privilege which they had enjoyed for centuries.

[43] Collet, *Raja Rammohun Roy*, p. 72.

The larger social context: the Young Bengal movement.

Within Rani Rashmoni's and Rammohun's lifetime (1772-1833), an epistemic shift had taken place by the emergence of a new generation of young natives (which would have included Mathur Biswas, Rashmoni's son-in-law), many of whom had been educated at the Hindu College and were immensely influenced by the new colonial, Western education system to the extent that they were referred to as "Young Bengal".[44] Dinesh Chandra Sen described Young Bengal as "the new generation" of Bengalis thoroughly "anglicized in spirit."[45] The latest intellectual developments in the Western world were transferred to Calcutta. Rammohun himself was critical of continuing with the indigenous system of education, and in a letter to Lord Amherst in 1823 criticized the government's decision to open a Sanskrit College as there was little merit in it. In fact, he hoped that the English government would devote the money to "employing European Gentlemen of talents and education to instruct the natives of India in Mathematical, Natural Philosophy, Chemistry, Anatomy and other useful sciences, which the Nations of Europe have carried to a degree of perfection."[46] Henry Derozio was a teacher at the Hindu College during these years, and was a great influence on his students. He was expelled from the college in 1831 partly because he was seen as too radical and dangerous for them.[47] Alexander Duff wrote after attending one such meeting of Derozio's students who were referred to as Derozians:

> The sentiments delivered were fortified by oral quotations
> from English authors. If the subject was historical,
> Robertson and Gibbon were appealed to; if political,
> Adam Smith and Jeremy Bentham; if scientific, Newton

---

[44] For more see Sumit Sarkar, "The Complexities of Young Bengal" in *A Critique of Colonial India* (Calcutta: Papyrus, 2000), pp. 29-48. Also Rosinka Chaudhuri, "Introduction," in *Derozio, Poet of India* (Calcutta: OUP, 2008), pp. lviii – lxxxi.

[45] D.C. Sen, *History of Bengali Language and Literature* (Calcutta: Calcutta University Press, 1911), p. 883.

[46] "Letter of Raja Rammohun Roy" in Sophia Dobson Collet's *Raja Rammohun Roy* (Calcutta, Sadharon Brahmo Samaj), p. 421. But this does not imply that Rammohun was not supportive of native education as he did set up a school which imparted Sanskrit education.

[47] See the letters regarding his resignation in *Derozio, Poet of India. The Definitive Edition.* pp. 319-326.

Sri Ramakrishna (1836-1886) and a nineteenth century subaltern.

> and Davy; if religious, Hume and Thomas Paine; if
> metaphysical, Locke and Reid, Stewart and Brown. The
> whole was frequently interspersed and enlivened by
> passages cited from some of our most popular English
> poets, particularly Byron and Sir Walter. And more than
> once were my ears greeted with the sound of Scotch
> rhymes from the poems of Robert Burns.[48]

A new system of colonial education had introduced processes of thinking amongst the natives that were described as radical: "Free-will, fore-orientation, fate, faith, the sacredness of truth, the high duty of cultivating virtue, and the meanness of vice, the nobility of patriotism, the attributes of God, and the argument for and against the existence of the deity as these have been set forth by Hume on the one side, and Reid, Dugald Stewart and Brown on the other, the hollowness of idolatory and the shams of priesthood were subjects which stirred to their very depths the young, fearless, hopeful hearts of the leading Hindoo youths of Calcutta."[49] Derozio introduced the latest European writers and philosophers to his students. The private world of their homes was Hindu for the most, whereas the public world of the college introduced them to systems of thought and social behaviour that were representative of contemporary Europe. Rani Rashmoni's son in law, Mathur Biswas, would have studied under such an environment, and subsequently influenced Rashmoni and Rajchandra.

Teachers and educators like D.L. Richardson made their way to the colony from England. Richardson was a teacher at the Hindu College, and published many volumes of prose and poetry in India; he was also the editor of the *Bengal Annual*—a yearly collection of poetry and prose that was published seven times between 1830 and 1836. But there would have been a dearth of books on Western philosophy, mathematics, science and literature that were needed to teach in classes and such needful books found their way to Calcutta in the most surprising way. Ships that came from England were loaded with books for Calcutta. It comes as a surprise that books for which the readership was uncertain were readily available in Calcutta. Emma Roberts describes such scenes of illiterate natives selling books to the Britishers:

---

[48] Alexander Duff, *India and India Missions* (Edinburgh: Whittaker, 1839), p. 614.

[49] Thomas Edwards, *Henry Derozio: Eurasian Poet, Teacher and Journalist*, quoted in Rosinka Chaudhury's *Gentleman Poets in Colonial Bengal. Emergent Nationalism and the Orientalist Project* (Calcutta: Seagull, 2002), pp. 25- 26.

> Immense consignments of books sometimes come out of
> Calcutta, through different mercantile houses, which are
> often knocked down for a mere trifle. American editions
> of works of eminence also find their way into the market
> at a very cheap rate. ... The inhabitants of Calcutta, or its
> occasional residents, can alone be benefited by the shoal of
> books brought upon the coast by a fleet more than
> ordinarily freighted with literary merchandise. ... At the
> Cape of Good Hope, the beach is said sometimes to be
> literally strewed with novels; an occurrence which takes
> place upon the wreck of a ship freighted from the
> warehouses of Paternoster Row; and certainly, in the
> streets of Calcutta, those who run may read; for books are
> thrust into palanquin- doors, or the windows of a carriage,
> with the pertinacity of the Jews of London, by natives,
> who make a point of presenting the title-pages and
> engravings upside down.[50]

From publishers in America and Paternoster Row, books made their way all the way to Calcutta. Most natives would not have cared for such books at this time in the history of print culture, unless they happened to be student of Hindu College or connected with Young Bengal. In this realm of print culture, there was an easy to-and-fro movement of texts from different parts of the world; ships were the bearers of these books. Alexander Duff wrote in 1839 that "some wretched bookseller in America, who—basely taking advantage of the reported infidel leanings of a new race of men in the East," sent to Calcutta "a cargo of that most malignant and pestiferous of all anti-Christian publications" [Tom Paine's *The Rights of Man*]; a single ship carrying a thousand copies landed, and with an increase of demand, the price of the book rose.[51] Booksellers did care for was money, but more importantly, the "wretched bookseller in America" who shipped *The Rights of Man* to Calcutta had other political-ideological aims than wanting to annoy Duff; Paine's works were instrumental in the American war of Independence, and the bookseller would have been keen to spread such an awareness in the newest colonies of Britain in the East. Thus, there was a

[50] Emma Robertson, *Scenes and Characteristics of Hindostan* (London: W. H. Allen, 1835), p. 8.

[51] Alexander Duff, quoted in Rosinka Chaudhuri's *Derozio*, "Introduction," p. Lxxiii.

Sri Ramakrishna (1836-1886) and a nineteenth century subaltern.

plethora of knowledge systems that existed in the early years of the nineteenth century in Calcutta.

We do not know how these varied systems of thought would have percolated through to the inner sanctum of Rani Rashmoni's household, but we have to accept that it did happen. How else can we explain the ease with which she was able to slip into becoming the manager and proprietor of Rajchandra's property after his death in 1868? With great diplomacy, she negotiated with the *bhadraloks*, the British government and the larger public in Calcutta, eventually going on to build the Dakshineshwar temple at a great expense.

Tapati Bharadwaj.

5 THE PUBLIC LIFE OF RANI RASHMONI.

The geo-spatial landscape of the city of Calcutta underwent many changes with the involvement of Rani Rashmoni and Rajchandra as they were involved in acts of public utility and philanthropy, building bathing *ghats* on the Ganga and roads across the city. It is within this context that we have to understand whether it is appropriate to refer to Rani Rashmoni as a subaltern. In most ways, she is outside the usual definition of the subaltern, where a large degree of "painstaking labor" is needed to establish "ethical singularity" with the subaltern. The overt life of Rani Rashmoni can be contained within the narrative of being very religious and gendered female, thus, locating her within the interiority of the house and the city; but we are unable to forget that she lived within the larger socio-cultural context of a westernized Calcutta. She was a subject in her own rights, and involved in self representation, thus problematizing Spivak's trenchant critique of 'feminists and native informants who occupy subject positions" and "are incapable of referring to the third world subaltern woman without patronage or presumption." Like the imperial subject who defines the subaltern as the other and uses her to complement the rational(western) self, Rani Rashmoni was able to conceptualize herself in the same fashion as the imperial subject or the native informant. Was this a result of the fact that Rajchandra and Rani Rashmoni interacted quite extensively with the Britishers? Her public presence is an anomaly for that time period, but allows her a sense of subjectivity, making self representation possible.

i. Philanthropy.

Rajchandra and Rashmoni were involved in many acts of charity and philanthropy which spread across the city of Calcutta; they were actively involved in constructing the "native" parts of the city. In 1823, when there were floods in Bengal, Rashmoni was generous in her assistance to the needy. In that same year, her father died and when she went to the Ganges to conduct the rites, she was made aware of the terrible conditions of the *ghats*. She requested her husband to construct a new *ghat* and a new road. Lord Bentinck did give permission and *Babu Ghat* and Babu Road were built. It is possible to argue that they ensured that they were involved in the creation of the physical landscape of Calcutta. In the list of their acts of philanthropy can be added that they donated money to a government library, and started a ferry service across the Beliaghata canal, and a pond was made in Talpukur, a suburb of Calcutta. Rani Rashmoni was an active participant in etching out the geo-social spaces in the city, and sometimes, working alongside the Britishers in order to conduct business. Not surprisingly, Rajchandra was given the title of "Rai Bahadur" by the British government in 1833. They were both ideal native subjects.

ii. Astute negotiator.

After the death of her husband in 1836, she was the custodian of his wealth. Prince Dwarkanath Tagore visited her and was willing to assist her by becoming the manager of her estate. He also owed her two hundred thousand rupees, and in lieu of that, he gave an estate of his. Eventually, Rani Rashmoni declined his offer and stated that her son in law would assist her. For a female subject and a widow living in the early nineteenth century in India, this act of negotiation, with an elite member of the *bhadralok* community, would have been quite an act of intelligence and sophisticated diplomacy.

iii. Legal theorist.

After the death of her husband, Rajchandra, she maintained a balance between her private life as a widow and was also involved in business. She was very religious. But what distinguishes her is her absolute grasp over legal theory. Once, during the celebration of Durga puja, her priests went to the Ganges in a musical procession; as it was early in the morning, and the music disturbed a Britisher who was sleeping. His complaint to the police was ignored and subsequently, Rani Rashmoni hired more musicians for the ceremony the next day. A court case was filed against her and she was fined fifty thousand rupees. Rani Rashmoni did pay the fine but barricaded a part of a public road which belonged to her. The government protested and eventually, the fine was returned and the barricade lifted.

iv. Involvement with the Britishers.

In 1838 Rani Rashmoni celebrated the car festival – Rathayatra – and a part of the events included inviting foreign dignitaries who were impressed at the proceedings. She also assisted the British government during the Sepoy Mutiny in 1857 with food and other needful. Such acts can only be construed as diplomacy on her part.

v. Public engagement through religion.

The Dakshineshwar temple by the Ganga in the suburbs of Calcutta was built at quite an expense. Work started in 1847 and continued for eight years. She spent 50, 000 rupees for the land, 160, 000 rupees for constructing an embankment along the river, and 900,000 rupees for the temple itself. An additional amount of 226,000 rupees was used to buy a property whose endowment would be used for maintenance of the temple. The temple would have been quite a grand affair at that time period for the newly developed fledgling city of Calcutta. Moreover, none of the other *bhadraloks* were involved in such an activity of temple building. It was here that Sri Ramkrishna lived most of his life.

There were no takers from amongst the Brahmin community to participate in her plans of offering cooked food to the deity; she was a *shudra* and could not do so. Sri Ramkrishna's brother, Ramkumar Chatterjee, who was living in the city and holding Sanksrit classes, did suggest a way out – if she formally gifted the temple to a brahmin, then this brahmin could offer cooked food to the deity and ensure that worship was done in the proper manner. Initially, Ramkumar joined the temple as a priest and subsequently, Ramakrishna also joined him.

Revisiting hybridity: Rani Rashmoni as a hybrid subject.

In order to understand the ease with which Rani Rashmoni was able to traverse multiple socio-cultural epistemic spaces, and be involved in a public manner within the landscape of a city at this time period, we have to arrive at a new interpretative model. How do we describe the engagement and emergence of a new cultural identity that was a result of the interaction between two cultures? The presence of the Britishers within India gave birth to a new breed of people, as is evident in the life of Rani Rashmoni. Like Rammohun, who blended Islamic, Hindu and British cultures, Rani Rashmoni also amalgamated many aspects of Indian and European cultures. But it is rather reductive to consider Rani Rashmoni as a one dimensional character, and instead we should arrive at newer models which consider her subjectivity as an inevitable process of cultural assimilation that inevitably takes place when two cultures interact.

Sri Ramakrishna (1836-1886) and a nineteenth century subaltern.

Postcolonial theory, on the other hand, suggests that hybrid identities are a recent phenomenon, a result of the metropole's interaction with the colonies. Catherine Hall, for example, argues that "unpacking imperial histories" means recognizing the insufficiency of core-periphery models and calls for analysis of the ways in which colonial subjects, goods, and ideas "criss-crossed" the globe.[52] Do we need to, therefore, always position Rani Rashmoni within this model of hybrid in-betweeness that is a result of the criss-crossing of ideas and colonial subjects? Such a theoretical position also underlines Antoinette Burton's scholarship. In *At the Heart of Empire, Indians and the Colonial Encounter in Late-Victorian Britain*,[53] she examines the narratives of three colonial subjects, Pandita Ramabai, Cornelia Sorabji and Behramji Malabari, in the metropole to exemplify the claim that colonialism was not a process that began in the metropole and expanded outward but was, rather, an historical moment "when new encounters within the world facilitated the formation of the categories of metropole and colony in the first place."[54] She goes on to state that her book presumes that:

> colonial identities have not historically been unified but have instead been fragmented across a variety of cultural axes, and that they have been determined in part in the social relations of the everyday—at the intersection, in other words, of the public and the private, the personal and the historical, the social and the political. … As we shall see, in domestic Victorian imperial culture the fact of colonialism shaped the terrains through which Indians walked and the spaces where they were required to elaborate the politics of their location(s) as colonial subjects. Most significantly, even the "givenness" of these terrains was in flux, negotiable, contestable— so that they were able to act as agents even while they were interpolated in particular ways by colonial discourses.[55]

---

[52] Catherine Hall, "Histories, Empires and the Post-Colonial Moment" in *The Post-Colonial Question: Common Skies, Divided Horizons*, ed. Iain Chambers and Lidia Curti (New York: Routledge, 1996), pp. 65-77. Also see *White, Male and Middle Class: Explorations in Feminist History* (London: Routledge, 1992).

[53] Antoinette Burton, *At the Heart of Empire, Indians and the colonial encounter in Late-Victorian Britain* (Berkeley: University of California Press, 1998).

[54] Nicolas Dirk, ed. "Introduction," in *Colonialism and Culture* (Ann Arbor: University of Michigan Press, 1992), p. 6.

[55] Burton, p. 15.

Burton's analysis suggests that the Indian colonial subject in the metropole
was at the interstices of many interlocking identities. A similar narrative
emerges in a different historical moment, when William Du Bois describes
the alienation of the African-American in a white society in antebellum
America. He writes that he was always shut out from the world of white
society by a "veil"; the black American "ever feels his two-ness – an
American, a Negro; two souls, two thoughts, two unreconciled strivings,
two warring ideals in one dark body."[56] He goes on to write:

> The history of the American Negro is the history of this strife, –
> this longing to attain self conscious manhood, to merge his double
> self into a better and truer self. In this merging he wishes neither of
> the older selves to be lost. He would not Africanize America, for
> America has too much to teach the world and Africa. He would
> not bleach his Negro soul in a flood of white Americanism, for he
> knows that Negro blood has a message for the world. He simply
> wishes to make it possible for a man to be both a Negro and an
> American...[57]

Du Bois draws attention to a notion of hybridity that suggests a heightened
degree of unreconcilability between two cultures. But, for the most,
hybridity as a concept has been monopolized by postcolonial theorists, and
is seen as a result of the racial, biological or cultural interaction between the
metropole and the colonies, or the colonizer and the colonized. I would, on
the other hand, hesitate to consider Rani Rashmoni and her phenomenal
capacity to absorb European culture, within this model of hybridity and
instead describe her as an inevitable socio-cultural emergence of the new
within imperial India. As had Rammohun and many others before him, in
their emulation of everything Islamic, Rani Rashmoni, despite being a
female subject in the early nineteenth century, marked the beginnings of
what was to be the new model of identity and behavior.

Conclusion.

Rani Rashmoni was Sri Ramakrishna's patron. She was involved in the
public world of business, and philanthropy to a very large extent. There is

---

[56] William Du Bois, *The Souls of Black Folks* (New York and London: Norton, 1999), p. 11.

[57] Ibid., p. 11.

Sri Ramakrishna (1836-1886) and a nineteenth century subaltern.

the very famous incident when Ramkrishna slapped her as she was thinking of a lawsuit while sitting in the temple and listening to his devotional songs. If Rani Rashmoni was all of the above, a hybrid, westernized female entrepreneur, under the disguise of conforming within the patriarchal mould, she was legitimized within mainstream Hinduism by the presence of Sri Ramakrishna.

www.ingramcontent.com/pod-product-compliance
Lightning Source LLC
Chambersburg PA
CBHW060644030426
42337CB00018B/3441